Don't Know Why 2
Seven Years 5
Cold Cold Heart 8
Feelin' The Same Way 11
Come Away With Me 14
Shoot The Moon 20
Turn Me On 17
Lonestar 22
I've Got To See You Again 23
Painter Song 26
One Flight Down 28
Nightingale 31
The Long Day Is Over 36
The Nearness Of You 38

Published by
Hal Leonard

Exclusive distributors

Hal Leonard
7777 West Bluemound Road
Milwaukee, WI 53213
Email: info@halleonard.com

Hal Leonard Europe Limited
42 Wigmore Street Maryleborne,
London, WIU 2 RN
Email: info@halleonardeurope.com

Hal Leonard Australia Pty. Ltd.
4 Lentara Court Cheltenham,
Victoria, 9132 Australia
Email: info@halleonard.com.au

Order No. AM990297
ISBN 978-1-84772-057-3
This book © Copyright 2007 by Hal Leornard

Music arranged and engraved by Artemis Music. Original PVG
transcriptions by Jack Long.

Photographer Clive Arrowsmith.
Photograph courtesy of Camera Press.

For all works contained herein:
Unauthorized copying, arranging, adapting, recording, Internet
posting, public performance, or other distribution of the music in
this publication is an infringement of copyright.
Infringers are liable under the law.

Printed in the EU.

www.halleonard.com

Don't Know Why

Words & Music by Jesse Harris

Con pedale

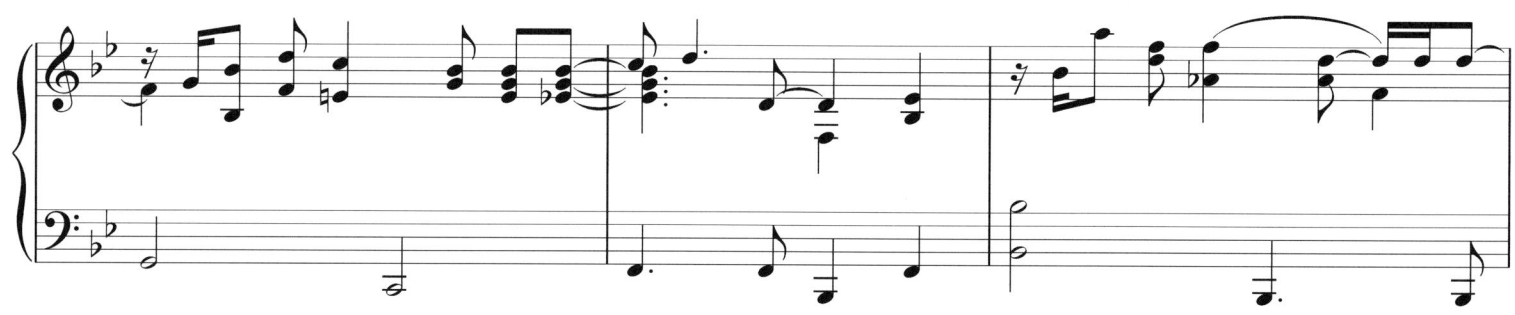

To Coda ✦

© Copyright 2002 Jesse Harris/Beanly Songs/Sony/ATV Songs LLC, USA.
Sony/ATV Music Publishing (UK) Limited.
All Rights Reserved. International Copyright Secured.

Seven Years

Words & Music by Lee Alexander

Gently ♩ = 126

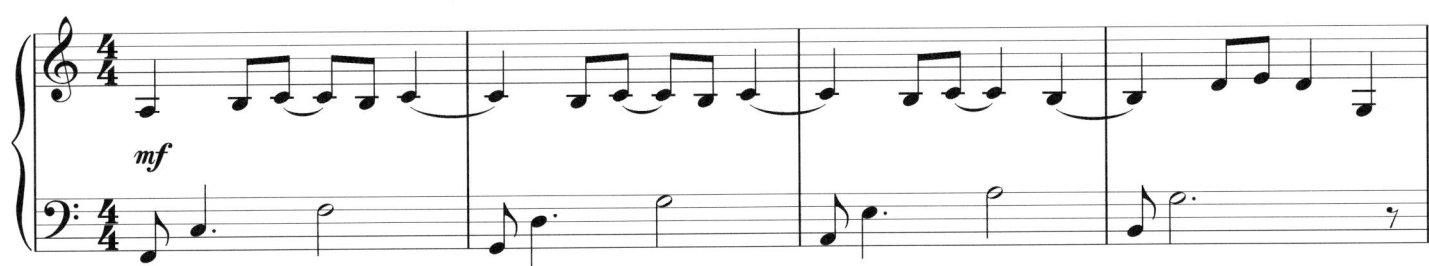
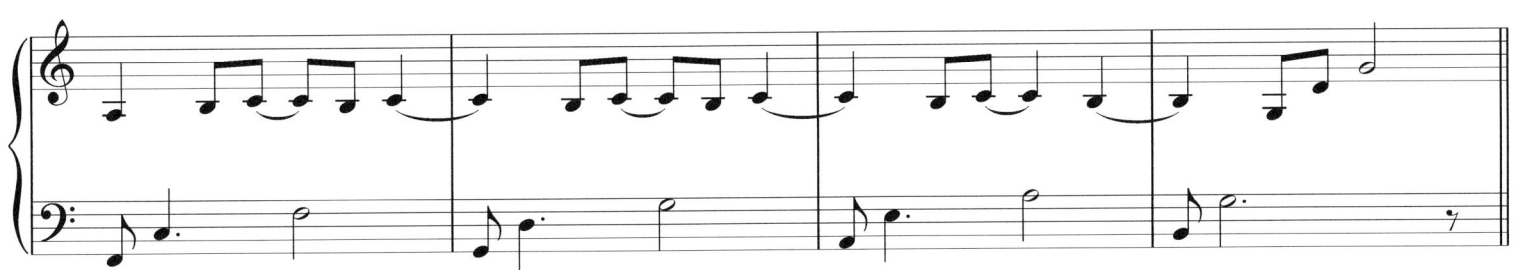

© Copyright 2002 EMI Blackwood Music Incorporated/Fumblethumbs Music, USA.
EMI Music Publishing Limited.
All Rights Reserved. International Copyright Secured.

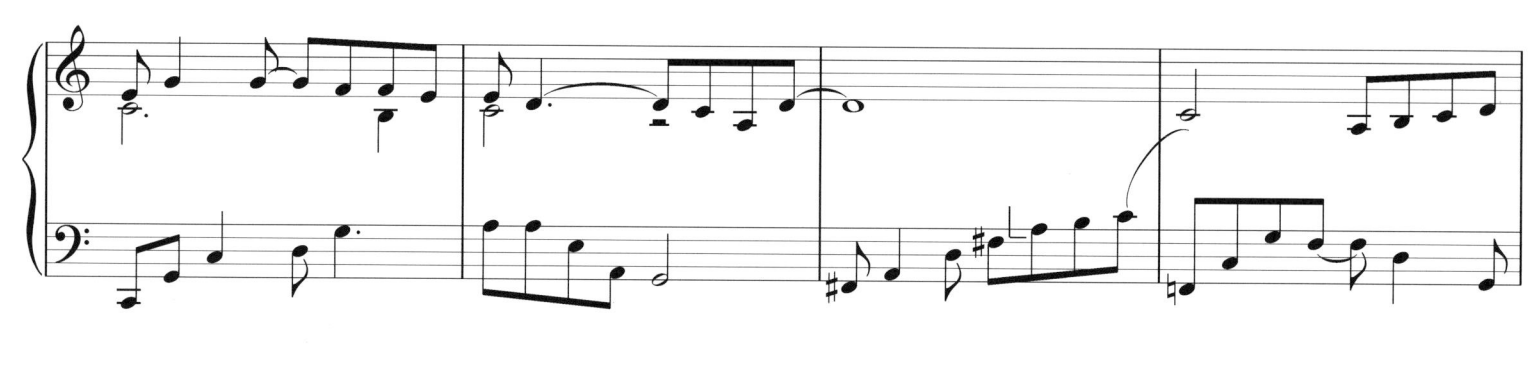

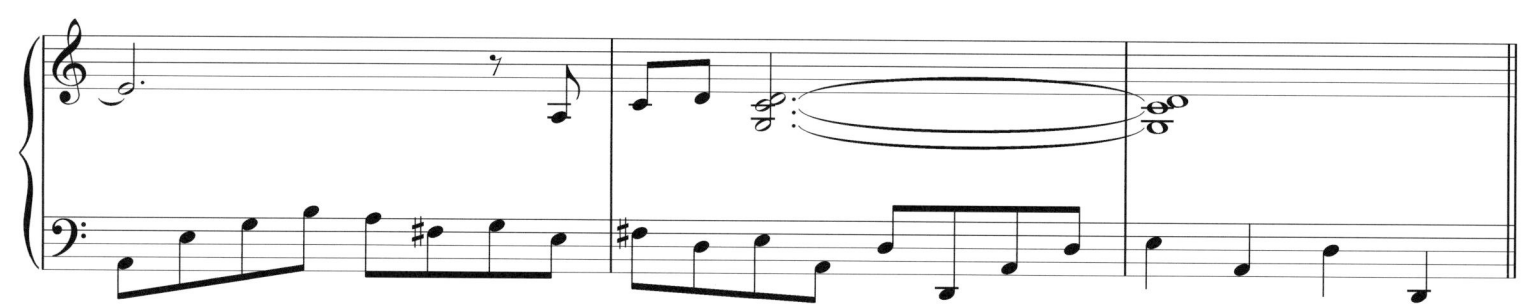

Cold Cold Heart

Words & Music by Hank Williams

Feelin' The Same Way

Words & Music by Lee Alexander

Tenderly ♩ = 108

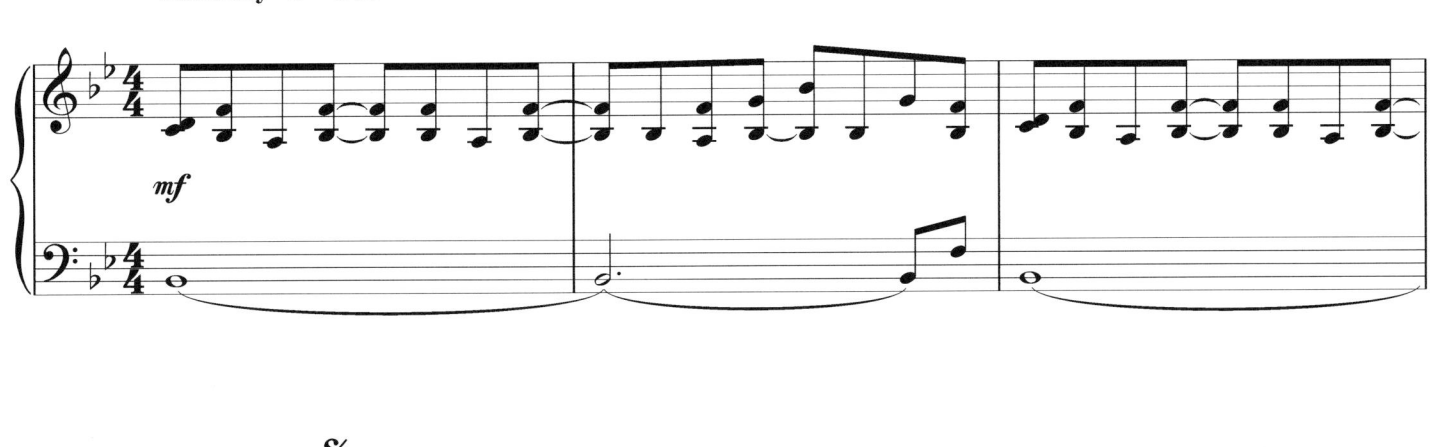

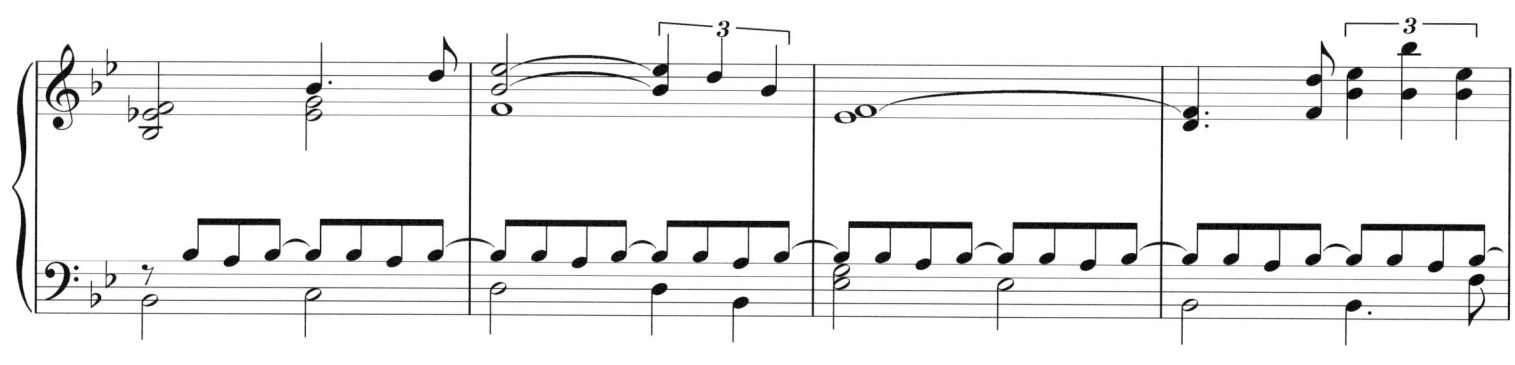

Come Away With Me

Words & Music by Norah Jones

Turn Me On

Words & Music by John D. Loudermilk

Shoot The Moon

Words & Music by Jesse Harris

Lonestar

Words & Music by Lee Alexander

© Copyright 2002 EMI Blackwood Music Incorporated/Fumblethumbs Music, USA.
EMI Music Publishing Limited.
All Rights Reserved. International Copyright Secured.

I've Got To See You Again

Words & Music by Jesse Harris

With a latin feel ♩ = 100

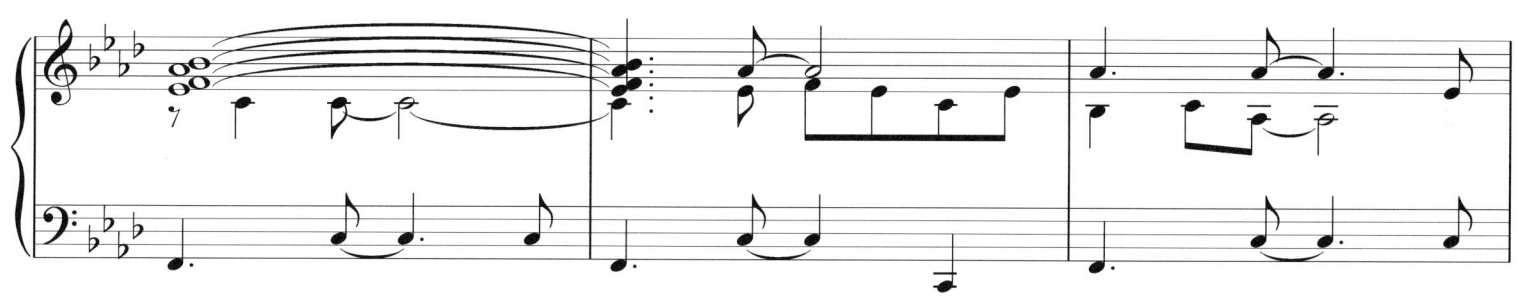
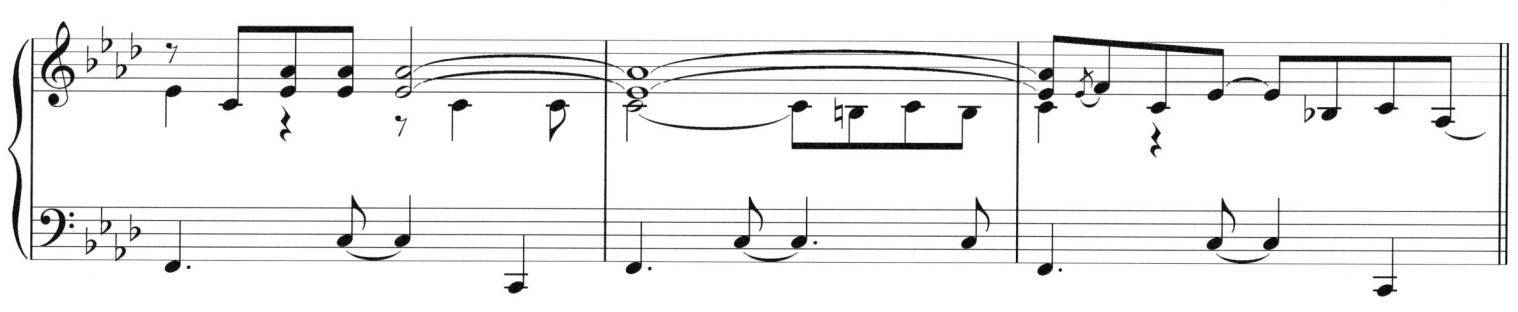

Painter Song

Words & Music by Lee Alexander & J. Hopkins

© Copyright 2002 EMI Blackwood Music Incorporated/Fumblethumbs Music/Writers Designee, USA.
EMI Music Publishing Limited (85%)/Bug Music Limited (15%).
All Rights Reserved. International Copyright Secured.

One Flight Down

Words & Music by Jesse Harris

Steadily ♩ = 66

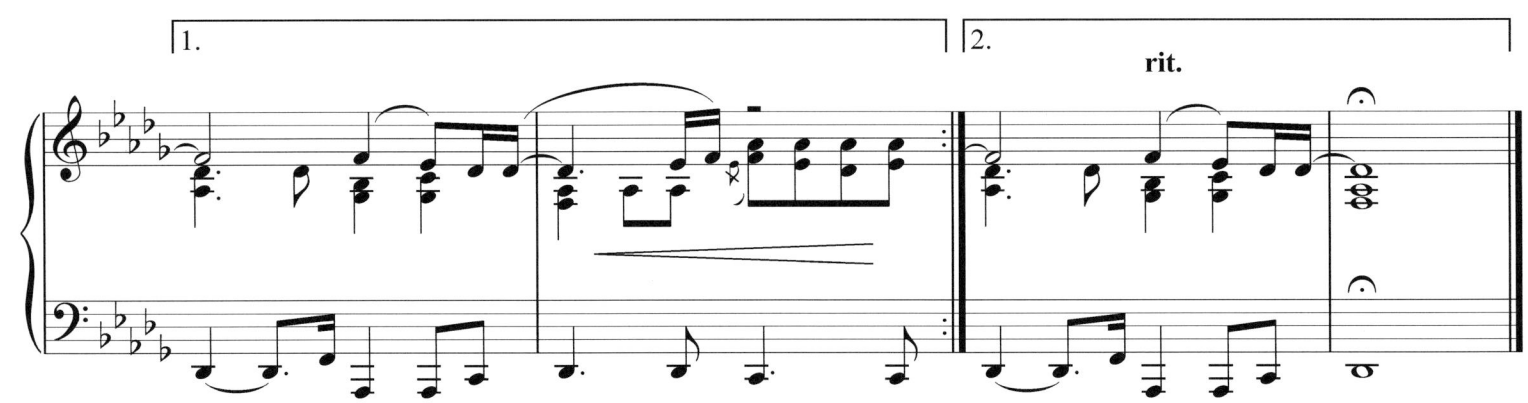

Nightingale

Words & Music by Norah Jones

Peacefully ♩ = 150

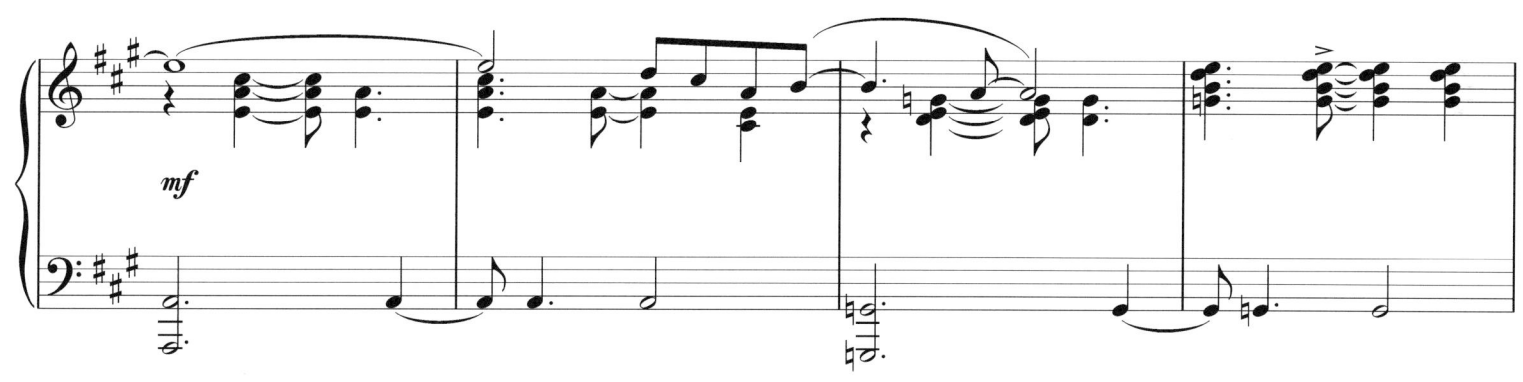

The Long Day Is Over

Words & Music by Norah Jones & Jesse Harris

Calmly ♩= 89

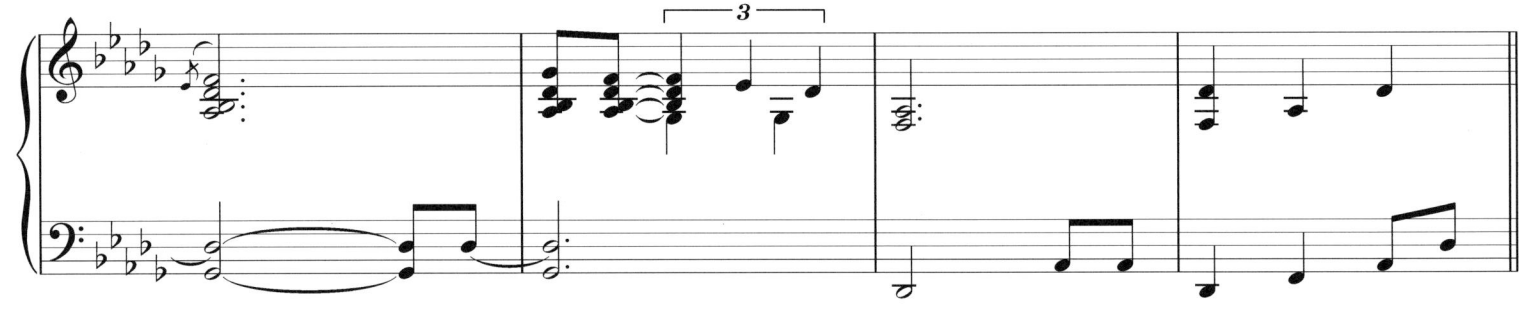

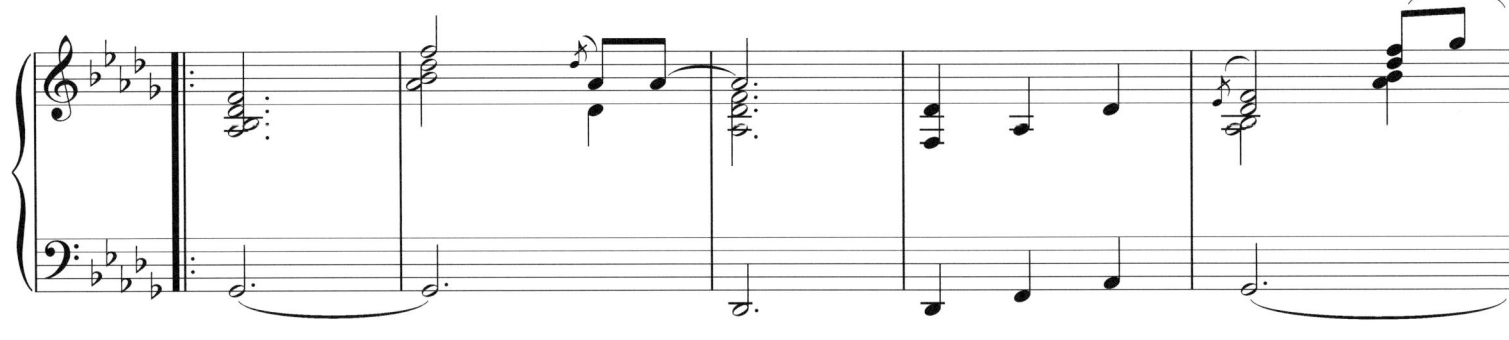

© Copyright 2002 EMI Blackwood Music Incorporated, USA/Writers Designee, USA/Muthajones Music LLC, USA.
Sony/ATV Music Publishing (UK) Limited (75%)/EMI Music Publishing Limited (25%).
All Rights Reserved. International Copyright Secured.

The Nearness Of You

Words by Ned Washington
Music by Hoagy Carmichael

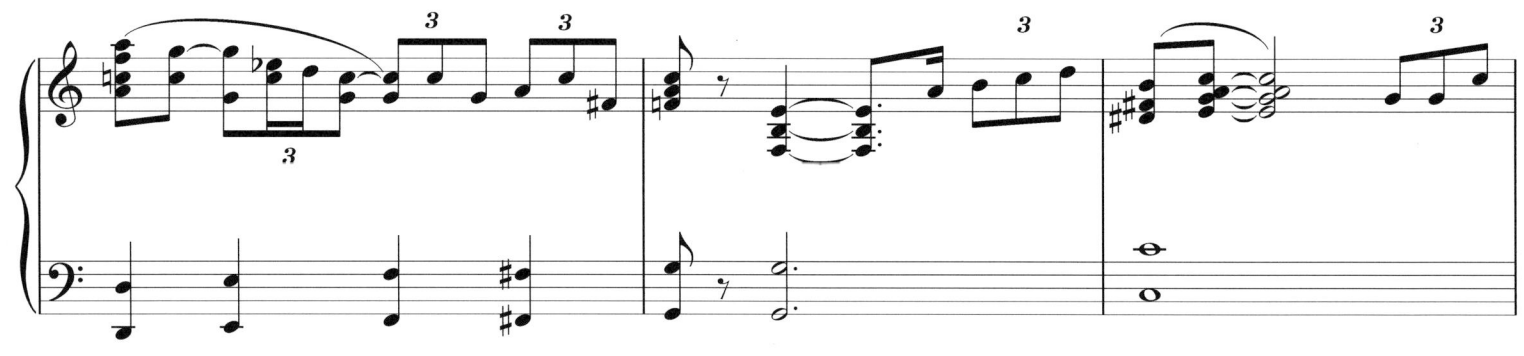
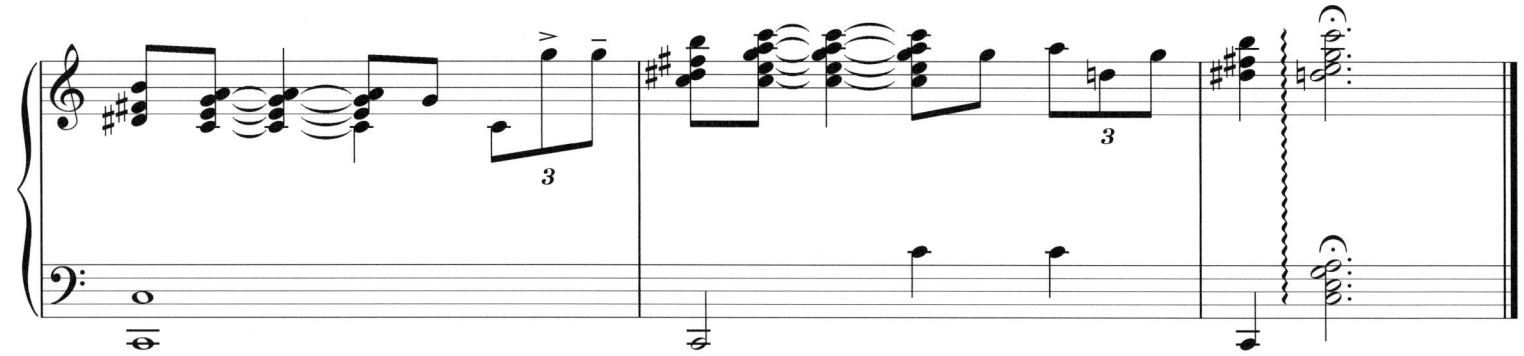